The

Joy

Habit

WONDERfully
WOVEN
encouraging women to live with purpose

The methods describe within this book are the author's personal thoughts. They are not intended to be a definitive set of instructions for this project. You may discover there are other methods and materials to accomplish the same end result.

DEDICATION

This book is dedicated to you; we pray that each day the joy of the Lord will overflow in your life.

The joy of the Lord
is our strength!
Neh. 8:10b
Janelle Keith
Lori Clapper

Why A Joy Habit?

Inspired by a couple of Wonderfully WOVEN writers, I decided that I needed to find a word for the coming year. This word would inspire me to greater things – one I could meditate on and learn from. So I began to conjure up my own list and, of course, told God what my word should be.

God, wouldn't mighty warrior or courageous be absolutely amazing words? I prodded over and over again. *Joy.* One simple three-letter word spoken in that familiar still, small voice. Nope. Not acceptable. That word wasn't nearly as cool as my ideas. What kind of word was "joy" anyway? I have joy, for heaven's sake. I love to laugh and relish good times. "I don't need work in that department, God."

But as the weeks went by, God impressed on my heart that He wanted to teach me how to find His joy in the mundane moments and even in the chaos, and oddly find strength in it. *The joy of the LORD is your strength!* Nehemiah 8:10. And not only was joy to be my word – but it was important enough to make it a habit.

I am truly grateful for each story shared within this devotional. Each writer shares how God taught her to find joy in many facets of life.

On behalf of each of us, we hope you are incredibly blessed by our very first 31-day devotional and that you find renewed strength through your new joy habit!

-Lori Clapper, founder of Wonderfully WOVEN

Day 1

Are You Laughing?

Lori Clapper

She is clothed with strength and dignity, and she laughs without fear of the future. PROVERBS 31:25

One of my favorite companies is Dove®. Yes, they do provide great beauty products that I use from time to time. But the thing I love most is their branding -- the way in which they celebrate beauty -- in all shapes, sizes and complexions.

As part of its marketing efforts, the company has released several thought-provoking short videos to prove its point. The most recent video, called *Dove Mirrors*, was released as part of the #beautyis campaign.

The video begins with women primping in mirrors, cell phones and window reflections -- stretching out forehead lines, sucking in tummies and frowning at their laugh lines. You can almost read their thoughts: *Well, this is as good as it will get....* Not too much laughing going on.

It then transitions to children catching their reflections in mirrors — making goofy faces, dancing around, laughing with pure delight at themselves. If you have kids, this will look very familiar. And it's very striking. *When was the last time you smiled back at your reflection?* Many times we get caught up and overwhelmed by life: finances, family, the fact that we don't look like our 20-year-old selves anymore. You may feel that it's no laughing matter. Or is it?

> *She laughs without fear of the future,* Proverbs says.

> *...when troubles of any kind come your way, consider it an opportunity for great joy. For you know than when your faith is tested, your endurance has a chance to grow.* James 1:2-3

> *"Don't be dejected and sad, for the joy of the LORD is your strength!"* Nehemiah 8:9-11

> *A cheerful look brings joy to the heart; good news makes for good health.* Proverbs 15:30

Need I say more? God makes it pretty clear in His Word that we must take joy in our journey. It's His plan. For His glory. To live our purpose here on Earth.

Sisters, whatever you are facing today, let's take a cue from our younger counterparts, and most importantly from our loving, all-knowing Creator. He came that we might have life....and live it to the full...no matter where you are right now. God is smiling down on you, when was the last time you smiled back? Why not make it today!

Pray

Lord Jesus, I don't understand why I get so down on myself some days. Help me to praise You even on bad hair days and days that I'm not feeling pretty or skinny. I am thankful that You have fearfully and wonderfully made me in Your image. Amen

Day 2

Living Like You're Redeemed

Casey Herringshaw

This means that anyone who belongs to Christ has become a new person. The old life is gone; a new life has begun!
2 CORINTHIANS 5:17

Redeemed. I didn't set out for this to be my One Word this year. Of course I know I'm redeemed. I've claimed Christ as my Savior. Asked Him into my heart and strive to live every day of my life with Him as my center focus.

I know all of these things inherently. So why do I have the word *redeemed* as my focus? Because I haven't claimed it yet. Not fully. Not in the deep, innermost parts of my being.

I keep letting Satan throwback everything from my past that Christ has told me is as far as the east is from the west. I keep letting the lies of the world—lies that tell me I'm inadequate, unworthy, undeserving and letting them fester within my heart and soul.

I get too caught up in what I did or said that I shouldn't have done or spoken. Forgetting that there is grace. That there is forgiveness. That there are second chances.

Instead, I focus on what I believe about myself. That I'm not good enough. And no, I'm really not. Neither are you. None of us will *ever* be *good enough*. If we had been good enough Christ wouldn't have had to come to earth. If we had been good enough Christ wouldn't have had to endure the painful trial and scourge.

If we had been good enough Christ wouldn't have had to suffer and die on the cross—the worst and most shameful death, He could have endured.

No, you and I, we'll never be good enough to deserve what Christ gave us. So I'm thankful it's not something I can ever earn. Somehow, though, it can seem harder to accept when it's a gift, can't it?

A gift is free. The only string attached to this gift is that we follow with whole abandon the Lord who loves us, wants to take care of us, and wants to mold us into the vessel that is poured out for Him. That's it. Love Jesus. Follow Him. Tell others about Him, which will only be a natural overflow by doing the previous two.

It's easy to turn our back on that gift and think that we'll never measure up. That we will never stop making the same stupid mistakes. That our worth is tied up in what other people think. Or what we've done. Or what we've said.

None...*none* of that matters. It was washed away in what Christ did on the cross. So why am I shameful of that? Because in turning my back on the redemption Christ offers, I'm communicating that I'm ashamed of what is being given to me—freely.

I like to think I've got it all together. It's not about having it all together. In fact, it's all about falling apart. And falling into Christ, to be completely and totally mended. Repaired. REDEEMED. I want to believe that this year. I want to make it an intrinsic part of my identity. The part that can't be separated or removed. Because Christ did that for me. Redeemed me. So I don't have to live in this fear. This feeling of worthlessness. This feeling of struggle. I am a NEW CREATION. Claimed by the Lover of my soul. And so are you.

Pray

God, a simple "thank You" seems hardly enough for what You did for me on the cross. I pray for Your strength, wisdom and grace as I strive to live like I am redeemed each day. Amen

Day 3

Childhood Memories

Karen Anna Vogel

And the streets of the city will be filled with boys and girls at play.
ZECHARIAH 8:5

Picking apples and berries with Nora, my elderly next-door neighbor. Seeing milkweed for the first time, breaking it apart to see feather-like stems float up. Sliding down grass on cardboard. These are my first awestruck memories of childhood. They've stayed with me because of the intense longing they produced; a longing to know God. C.S. Lewis, in his book, *Surprised by Joy*, tells of similar situations and images embedded in his heart.

He wrote, *"If I find in myself desires which nothing in this world can satisfy, the only logical explanation is that I was made for another world."*

These childhood moments did not satisfy me. They whet my appetite to know God. They were strong enough to withstand life's drama until at the age of eighteen - when I met Joy himself: Jesus. He gives a joy no one can take away. (John 16:22) It's a settling in the heart, knowing that God's love will see me through, not a temporary happiness that fades. So, if our childhood memories can make us yearn for God, is there something to nurture a childlike nature? Lewis read Beatrix Potter's *Peter Rabbit* books his entire life.

To be honest, I was relieved to discover this because I do, too. I have a granddaughter who loves to play make-believe. My coffee table is a place where she makes purple cakes with pink icing. She serves it to me and I take a bite and immediately put in an order for a pink cake with yellow icing with a cherry on top. With a few stirs in her imaginary bowl, she spins around and says, "Grandma, here's your cake." I am so rejuvenated.

So am I saying to play? Yes. A thousand times yes.

Laugh, too. You can't be stressed out and laugh at the same time. You can't smile and be stressed at the same time. Does the Bible say to play? Yes!

And the streets of the city will be filled with boys and girls at play. Zechariah 8:5

This is the reward of those whose sins are forgiven. *Play!* Play means to celebrate. I think Jesus loved to celebrate. His first miracle was at a wedding.

There is nothing in this world that can satisfy, like Lewis says, but there are "joy pointers." For me, a little girl leads me…especially when she's dressed like a princess with long flowing yarn hair. I feel like fairy dust has been sprinkled on me after our playtime, and I'm calm. Calm and still enough to hear the voice of God say:

For the LORD your God is living among you. He is a mighty savior. He will take delight in you with gladness. With his love, he will calm all your fears. He will rejoice over you with joyful songs. Zephaniah 3:17

Pray

God, help me to relax today. I pray for just a few moments to push adult responsibilities aside, so I can enjoy life…and just play. Amen

Day 4

Finding Joy During the Holidays

Tara Norman

The thief's purpose is to steal and kill and destroy. My purpose is to give them a rich and satisfying life. JOHN 10:10

Christmastime is my favorite time of the year. I love the joy and magic of Christmas. No other holiday brings me quite as much joy. However, for many, this holiday brings sadness. Perhaps some are grieving. Maybe memories of the past come back to haunt you this time of the year. *Satan* is a joy stealer. God's word says that it is his task: *The thief's purpose is to steal and kill and destroy. My purpose is to give them a rich and satisfying life.* Satan will come in many ways: through a rude phone call, your toddler's untimely tantrum, the never-ending tasks that have to be checked off before Christmas, bills, or unforeseen emergencies. I want to share with you five different ways to help you find your joy again when the enemy steps in this season.

Light a candle and play some Christmas music. A candle works if you are at home. If you work, find an essential oil that you like or an Airwick to use at your workplace. Sometimes engaging different senses helps melt away that stress and helps you hit the re-start button.

Pray. In reality, I do numbers 1 and 2 together especially if I have two children melting down at the same time. In these moments I address needs, pray aloud for God to bring peace to our home, turn on Christmas music, light my favorite candle and sit on the floor to play. I pray the distraction will be enough to calm everyone down.

Plan ahead. I find stress and frustration can sometimes be avoided if we had planned ahead. Set a date to get your Christmas cards in the mail. Budget for gifts and know when you will be buying what. Plan ahead for the teacher's gifts.

Give yourself permission. Give yourself permission to buy cupcakes instead of staying up until 3 am to make dozens for your kid's class parties. Give yourself permission to duck out of some holiday parties to spend time at home. Sometimes we are the ones that put the most pressure on ourselves, and we have to give ourselves permission to just let it go.

Give. It really is true that it feels better to give than to receive. If you find yourself making a coffee run because it's been that kind of day, pay for the person behind you too. Put together some bags to give out when you pass all of those who are in need along the highway this year. Giving to others is a sure way to help you find your joy again.

The devil is clever, but not unstoppable. We know the end of the story; we win. As we remember and celebrate the coming of our Lord and Savior, the devil is going to try to steal your comfort and joy. Don't let him. Be ready for battle this year.

Pray

Lord, I thank You for your Son and for His life so I might know You. Help me to be ready for the thief who comes to steal my joy this Christmas. I thank You and praise You. Amen

Day 5

Finding Joy in the Midst of Anger

Tara Norman

The tongue can bring death or life... PROVERBS 18:21

Ever been in a fight with your husband and tried to pray for him? Several times in our twelve-year marriage, my husband and I have been at a stalemate about something, and I have been madder than a hornet at him. In those times, he will grab my hands and say let's pray. I briefly, secretly rebel because I know the moment his mouth opens to ask God for help -- all of that anger will vanish. His simple Godly leadership to go humbly before the Lord brings me joy in the midst of my anger.

Those heated words I am yelling at him in my head turn into heated tears. And instead of punishing my husband with a tongue-lashing, I start praying for wisdom and guidance over him and myself.

When you give into the fleshly desire to tear your husband down, you are damaging the very person you love, the one you devoted your life to -- for better or worse. Whether you call him a name or shame him in that moment, you are changing who they are. You can speak life or death into those you love by the words you use.

There was a study done by Dr. Masaru Emoto that showed this exact thing. He would use music, pictures, videos, and words to create a reaction in water to show that it has a memory. After he had exposed the water to music or words, he would crystallize it. The crystals were a mirrored image of what they were exposed to it in water form. If you have time, look up the study on YouTube.

My point is God wasn't using a simple analogy when he said in Proverbs, *Death and life [are] in the power of the tongue...* (Proverbs 18:21) As with all things in the Bible, *it's the absolute truth.*

Today, when the devil lures you in with thoughts of anger, reel yourself back to The One who flung the stars into the very heavens, and ask for help. Your prayer will be *sweet to the soul and healthy for the body.* (Proverbs 16:24)

Pray

Lord, help my words to be healing and sweet to the soul. Help me to speak life and bring joy to others every time I open my mouth today.

Amen

FOOTNOTE

WEB ADDRESS TO THE STUDY COMPLETED BY
DR. MASARU EMOTO
https://www.youtube.com/watch?v=tavzsjcbtx8

Day 6

Finding Joy in the Training

Tara Norman

Direct your children onto the right path, and when they are older, they will not leave it. PROVERBS 22:6

Life for us has become so much more interesting since our fourth child came into the picture. It seems when things get chaotic they get really out of control, ridiculous chaotic. Simple trips do not exist anymore. It does take a full hour to get out the door now. We can no longer talk in the van because we have four kiddos who talk louder and louder daily.

Oh the lessons in motherhood "number four" has been teaching me. He is so independent, headstrong, and determined. While he may be the baby, he acts more like a first-born. It was him who decided to move to a toddler bed, him who decided it was time to crawl and walk, him who decided he was going to learn to count and say his ABC's, and him who decided it was time to move on from diapers.

He keeps me running ALL DAY LONG. Like ragged. Like I can't even stay awake past 9:30 PM ragged. The three kids before him were on a schedule. I put them through "meet your milestone" boot camp. Along came number four and he rocked my world. I humbly realized that God was temporarily moving me from my position as trainer to the one being trained.

I have sought after God more in motherhood than any other time in my life. I have only been a mother for 10 of my almost 40 years. One of the biggest lessons I am learning repeatedly in motherhood is, *Direct your children onto the right path*, Proverbs 22:6.

Oftentimes, I find that *I am the child* that is being trained by God. I am consistently being pushed to my limits in motherhood so our Abba can train *me* and show *me* that I alone cannot fill this role, that I need Him. I am brought to my knees daily seeking Him, asking for grace, more patience, and more wisdom.

Every morning I get back up for another day of training. I find peace and joy knowing that even if my day didn't go as planned, the best Daddy in the world whose grace and patience is never-ending is training me. I will get back up again tomorrow with mercies anew and try again.

Pray

Lord, I thank You for Your mercies that renew daily. Help me to hear and recognize Your voice as You train me and mold me in the way I should go. Amen

I Hope You Dance

Casey Herringshaw

You have turned my mourning into joyful dancing. You have taken away my clothes of mourning and clothed me with joy…

PSALM 30:11

I'm certainly not the first one to come up with this phrase. In fact, I have Lee Ann Womack to thank for first stringing together those four words into a song. A song that sticks in my head and strings forth from my car radio and work computer. *I hope you dance.*

In words different from the song:

I hope you take time to enjoy the sunrise.

The sunset.

I hope you take time to appreciate the smile of a child,

The warmth of the sunshine.

The feel of grass between your toes.

The laugh of a loved one.

I hope you take the time in the word of God.

The gift of His Son.

The wonder of His resurrection.

The power of His salvation.

The depth and wonder of His love.

We get sucked into the hard or mundane things in our day-to-day lives. I'm just as guilty of this. What is on the to-do list that I must get done today, hopefully before the clock strikes midnight, so I actually get a full night's rest? (yeah right, more like a wink or two before it's time to rise to an all-too-early alarm). I get caught up in the tangled web of to-do's, drama, frustrations and all too light joy.

When was the last time I took a bit of time to soak in the joy that surrounds me? Instead of rushing from one thing to another, wishing for one aspect or another of my life to be behind me and regardless of everything—good or bad—in my life, and took time to dance? My friends will laugh at me for that last line. Because, honestly? I can't dance. Not one step.

I'd love to learn, but haven't taken the time (are you sensing a theme here?) to actually figure out what a rhythm is from what I hear in my ears to what comes out of my feet. Life is more than to-dos and to-dones. Life is more than the struggles that can often fill our days to all-consuming overwhelming.

Life is about finding JOY. I have to admit; this has not been my strong point lately. Loneliness for faraway family and discouragements of varying arrays have left me drained and trudging from one task to another.

Rushing in the morning only to rush through the day to get home and rush through my extra-curricular activities to rush to bed so I can sleep as well as I can before rushing into wakefulness the next morning and starting it all over again.

This isn't the way God called us to live life. Because even in the midst of busyness—maybe even busyness that He has called you to pick up during this season of your life—we should never forget the reminder that life is only given to us one breath at a time.

You're not promised five minutes from now, let alone five years from now. Don't put off until tomorrow what you have wanted to soak in today.

When you look back on your life, it's not going to be the massive accomplishments you've completed, it'll be the little joys, the ways you touched someone's life that stand out to you the most.

So I hope you dance.

I hope you remember - in every single one of those two-steps, square dance, slow dance, salsa moves - just how much joy, life and love surrounds you.

No matter your circumstances. You just have to take the time to look.

Pray

Dear Lord I know that in so many of life's circumstances, I have "two left feet." I let my troubles bring me down and hold me back. I pray that You give me the strength and joy to dance today, no matter what the day may bring. Amen

Day 8

In the Storm

Janelle Keith

But the LORD's plans stand firm forever;
his intentions can never be shaken. PSALM 33:11

I didn't know I would see joy once I heard her pain. She was so young when her mother died. She was like any other five-year-old with a hurting heart, she was full of pain, tears and questions. But now there was one bigger problem she would face. In a matter of moments, she had to grow up. She became a double orphan at the small age of five.

I barely remember when I was five years old. What could it possibly feel like to lose your security, your caregiver at such a young, tender stage?

How would that loneliness hit your soul? My mind drifts back to that long hallway from my Kindergarten school days. I cried as I watched my mom walk away down the long cold hallway after she dropped me off in my new blue plaid dress and velveteen extra-wide buckled shoes. I felt so alone at the age of five.

Others saw me cry and called me a baby. That day I didn't care; I wanted to bolt after my only known source of love. My heart wanted to remain tied to her apron strings forever. I was known as a "momma's girl." I remember that feeling of abandonment, the feeling of being the only one who couldn't handle a half day of separation from my mom, that feeling of emptiness and loss.

Tilly told me of her journey of rescue. Becoming a double orphan at the age of five, she had no one to turn to for refuge. I can't wrap my mind around that process of what to think or how to respond to her. But yet in her story she shared how she was found. She gave thanks for someone reaching out to her and taking her in. Safety in a small home for orphans became her refuge. God's infinite love became her buoy in endless ocean of mixed emotions. She was not forgotten or abandoned now. She was introduced to her Jesus, now her Savior, and He became her new place of joy. Let that truth settle in for a moment. A young girl at five, just lost her entire world as she knew it. And then someone introduced her to Jesus.

My heart melts at the saving knowledge of Jesus Christ and the power of salvation. God had that moment of loss all planned out for Tilly, including a refuge answer in place before the loss was on her horizon. Knowing there was going to be pain, loss, and tears but planning for her rescue *for his intentions can never be shaken.* (Psalm 33:11)

I am so thankful for God and His plans for us and for our refuge. In the middle of Tilly's pain, reeling from the loss of the one who gave her life, God brought her new life at five years old, and coupled that with an important life skill.

He taught her to joyfully praise. Her joy-filled smile had to be God given to comprehend the magnitude of her praise.

She later wrote these words in response to her Refuge:

"Lord, oh God,

You are the King of Kings

You are everything, my life...

I'm gonna praise you Lord,

I'm gonna praise you Lord,

I'm gonna praise you Lord,

For the rest of my life."

One that praises with joy in the middle of her storm. Her testimony spoke deeply to my heart to heal my heart. So thankful for the plans of the Lord and His awesome rescues that He gives us on a daily basis.

Pray

Lord, I am so thankful that we have a place in Your heart for eternity. So thankful that it moves my heart to praise and have a deep abiding joy. Yes, Lord..."I'm gonna praise You Lord...for the rest of my life with... JOY!" Amen

Day 9

Joy Amidst the Rocky Waves

Julia Reffner

Instead, be very glad--for these trials make you partners with Christ in his suffering, so that you will have the wonderful joy of seeing his glory when it is revealed to all the world. 1 PETER 4:13

White flecks of snow stuck to my father's yellow and black jacket we had christened as his "bumblebee coat". The smell of French press coffee was unable to mask the yellowed smell of IV fluid. CANCER. The words were bitter and stuck to the tip of my tongue. The joy of my college years punctuated in short staccato breaths with hospital visits.

Five years later, I sat bolt upright in my bed, my body sensing the last breath had exited my father's lungs. My own rapid successions of air captured in a lunch paper bag. Numbness entered my heart. In the months that followed, God's breaths filled in my empty deflated lungs. His words fed my undernourished mind. So many other sorrows fill our minds and hearts. The loss of dear friends, miscarriage, infertility, financial loss, life's endless cycle of endings and beginnings.

Jesus in us, the only hope of our soul, the endless anchor of strength and courage that enables us to stand through what the unbelieving world looks at as impossible. The Presence holding our hand, just waiting for us to climb out of the boat again, when all we see is a long crescendo of waves, threatening to hold us underneath with what we think of as their strong power. Forgetting that the Captain of our ship is the Man of Sorrows, the One who calms the sea and holds all of nature in His power.

He comforts us as the waves crash around our boat, calming the deeper storm that threatens inside us. The storm of our fears, crimson-sin stains, guilt, shame, the emotions that threaten to capsize us, all that holds us captive, threatening shipwreck.

The joy comes in the midst of our sorrows when we step out into the boat, finding His grace is enough to carry us to shore when our body collapses under the pain. His mercy is more than sufficient to push each arm and leg stroke by stroke to the finish line. His breath into our lungs sustains us when we run out of air.

Joy is fulfilled when God strengthens our arms to carry another body, weak with sin, burdened by the same sorrows we face to shore. When we give a cup of cold water to refresh their hurting soul, out of the overflowing spout the Spirit has filled. Then our joy is complete when we join the team of angels on the celestial shore, singing His praises, and hear "well done, thou good and faithful servant." Until then, hold fast to joy.

Pray

Lord, help us bring joy to a hurting world to show a reflection of the joy that is to come in the heavenly realm. Amen

Joy at Exit 15

Angie Kay Webb

A cheerful heart is good medicine, but a broken spirit saps a person's strength. PROVERBS 17:22

Joy can be found at any point of the day or night, but we must first be on the lookout. This world can be so full of busyness that we can miss the simple things of life that bring us joy. Joy can be found in the everyday things such as a sweet baby's face, a kiss from a loved one or seeing the beauty of a colorful rainbow. Joy can come in many forms, but the one true joy is living free.

For many years I struggled with fear, anxiety and agoraphobia. Yet in 2012 God totally set me free. From a very young age to the age of 45 years old I lived in fear of traveling because this required being away from home, which was my comfort zone. Fear can be such a horrible feeling, and if you have never experienced it you should count yourself blessed. During all of those years of struggle, I never truly believed that the fear would ever leave my life -- yet today I am finding JOY at Exit 15 or any Exit that I find myself taking as my husband and I travel.

Exit 15 holds a special place in my heart because this was a point on the road that I would never drive past. Then one-day joy appeared there as I drove past to the next exit in my journey to freedom and joy.

Joy can be found in the biggest and smallest places of life. Joy can be found even at EXIT 15. Joy is a choice.

What is holding you back from having JOY in your life? Is it something from your past? Or a fear of the future? Self-doubt? People pleasing?

God sees you and hears your heart's cry. God hears all your prayers and wants you to ask Him for anything; even for JOY to return to your heart and life. Joy, peace and love. God's desires these for each of His children.

Pray

God, I trust Your promise that You never leave me nor abandon me.

Thank You for going before me as I feel stretched beyond

my own limits. Amen

Day 11

True Joy for Each Season

Janelle Keith

The LORD is my strength and shield. I trust him with all my heart.
He helps me, and my heart is filled with joy. I burst out in songs of
thanksgiving. PSALM 28:7

It was a season of caring for my aging parents, when it was time to pack for a trip to Africa. How could I go and spread the Christmas joy to children, when I was in the middle of a joyless situation in my family?

Isn't everyone supposed to have joy in December? At least I thought I was the only one who got left out of the sprinkle and sparkle the joyous Christmas season brings. I had missed the holiday memo and didn't catch the shopping fever. It was actually…. depressing.

The health of my parents was declining, and my siblings and I had to make some tough decisions regarding their care. When you have the roles reversed in your family after 60 + years of marriage, well there is no joy in watching your parents fall apart. Those days were filled with lots of tears and talks about what to do, the best plan, educating ourselves about many diseases and arming ourselves with the best wisdom we could grasp.

The process of caring for our aging parents was not filled with joy. However, there's something about looking for joy that sustains you -- even when you can't feel or taste it in your daily life. There's an underlying current of happiness that begs the invitation to find joy as it slowly ebbs in your inner spirit. There is a peace that lays low and rises to the top when you need assurance. There are banks of trust that border your decision-making. There is a silent hope that whispers at you to nudge you in the right direction. There is an unspoken trust in the professional's wisdom coupled with answered prayers that brings understanding when words and questions escape you. We did feel the Lord's hand in our decisions.

So in a way there were some joy seeds that were taking root, germinating slowly before I could see them. Those joy seeds were loaded in my heart when I packed for the upcoming African Christmas parties.

Once on the plane, the joy of leaving the stress behind quickly took its place in my heart. It was a relief to just think about something else for about a week. I rested on the peace I felt that my parents would be okay until I returned. Our team landed on the ground about 24 hours later, and joy was immediately felt within the energy of the staff that had prepared the parties for the children. Joy was spilling out of every pore.

Each of us was assigned to a party station for the festivities. And it just so happened that the Lord placed me into the party station that required the most joy "output": the dance and cake station. The more joy I spread to the Children, the more I felt God building in me. Can you see how God planned for my joy needs?

At my weakest point, God supplied the joy I needed. I sensed His true joy in the celebration of the season. I let go to let Him cultivate more joy than I could hold on that African party ground. I packed it back up and brought it home, spreading it to everyone I could. It was such a great gift at such a desperate time for me.

Joy received from the Lord is the most sincere feeling. Joy fortifies and strengthens your soul and is second to God's perfect love. It's a fruit that can be enjoyed in every season!

Pray

Abba, thank You for Your joy that penetrates deep into my soul, no matter what my circumstances are. Let me always believe that Your joy is my strength. Amen

Day 12

Joy in the Gift

Lori Clapper

Give generously…not grudgingly, for the LORD your God will bless you in everything you do. DEUTERONOMY 15:10

It was a great night's sleep. One of those deep, peaceful sleeps you don't want to end (and are way too rare these days). But early that morning, in my bleary-eyed semi-consciousness, I was interrupted by a still small voice.

"The voice" was telling me to give a certain amount of money to a dear friend who had not only helped me in ministry, but was pursuing a new venture herself. Her cheerful, "just-trust-God-it-will-work-out" attitude is the perfect balance for my naturally panicky, deadline-driven, micromanaging self.

But trusting God with finances has never been easy for me. So following that quiet moment was a heart palpitation.

Is that really you, God? Maybe it was that third slice of pizza I had eaten the night before.

I've heard plenty of stories about God's economy and have even seen blessing my own life. But at times when the budget numbers don't balance, my natural instinct is to freak out. There'd be nothing I wouldn't do for my friend. But still I argued. Really God? Money is tight right now.

God spoke it again. *Give.* I kept ignoring it. That night I was shopping online. And was about to dump a decent amount of money on something that was certainly not a necessity. I tried several times to complete the purchase, but my computer kept freezing. But…. God. *You won't think twice about spending money on these frivolous things. Do you love me more than these? Then give.*

Ouch. Yep. He got my attention that time. When God calls, I guarantee He won't let you forget. For two days, I had wrestled with God. My lack of trust put my heart in knots. But as it says in our key verse, *Your heart shall not be grieved when you give to him.* My heart was more grieved by *not* giving! I wrote the check and gave it to her the next night. Blessing her brought unspeakable joy to my spirit.

What is God calling you to give today? Do you feel that you should start tithing to your church? Maybe to bless someone you know who is in need? Or perhaps He's calling you to give of your talents and gifts in a new way. That gentle nudge is God speaking to you. Take it from me…. don't ignore it. Give with joy, even when you think you can't. God will bless your works.

Pray

Lord, I know I need to trust You more, especially with money. When times are tough, I hold on too tight. But You have said in Your Word that You love a cheerful giver. Today, I put my finances in Your hands. Help me to have joy in giving to others. Amen

Joy in the Unknown

Angie Kay Webb

The Lord is always faithful even when we don't understand the path we are facing. Often the joy we feel may need to be forced on some levels because we just are not "feeling" the joy of the Lord in our hearts and lives. I certainly can attest to that in my own life after losing my grandparents to a murder/suicide. Nothing made sense after that fateful day in 1996. But even in the unknown, God once again allowed me to find joy, peace and purpose. It wasn't an overnight process but a long, difficult, painful process. Sometimes I just wanted to throw in the towel and stay stuck in the pain, but God wants us to find joy, love and peace again.

Reminder: JOY=Jesus + **O**thers + **Y**ourself

Focus on Him first, then others and then yourself. Everything will fall into place.

It can happen for you, too, even when you are facing despair, heartache, loss and pain. God is always faithful to help us find HIM again if we only ask in prayer. Prayer connects us to the heart of the Father and allows us to know Him and His plan on a deeper level.

Prayer is our lifeline to once again find joy in our hearts and lives. Joy is possible even in the unknowns of life.

Pray

Lord, I come to You today to ask for You to hear my desperate cries during the "unknowns" of life. As I face the new day, help me to remember that You are always there — even when I don't feel the joy of the Lord. You have not left and are just waiting for me to ask for Your help. Joy is possible again, and I am waiting for that day to arrive soon.

Help me to see the joy in the small things of life. Amen

Day 14

Joy is a Verb

Dr. Andrea Hazim

Honor and majesty surround him; strength and joy fill his dwelling.
1 CHRONICLES 16:27

Have you ever noticed the "IF – THEN" statements in God's Word? It's as if the Holy Spirit is saying, "Take note!" IF **JOY** is in His dwelling place, THEN how do we get there? IF we draw near to Him, THEN the Father will lay His hand upon us, welcoming us into His presence. I can't think of a better place to be!

Powerful is your arm! Strong is your hand! Your right hand is lifted high in glorious strength. Psalm 89:13

Can you picture Esther, when the King's scepter is extended in favor of her approaching the King (also her husband)? Our Heavenly King's arm and hand are truly our source for everything. Esther found favor and experienced JOY as a result of her actions. When we choose to go before the King, which takes a certain humility and courage, JOY is demonstrated as a verb.

Like Esther, IF you will actively align yourself with the King's presence, THEN you will experience the Father's touch.

He desires to reach into this earthly dimension to fortify your spirit, which transforms your heart, mind, and even your body! Have you ever experienced God like that? Would you like to? His loving touch reprograms our mental DNA. Eventually, like we know our own names, we understand that we are not really human beings at all, but Kingdom beings; citizens of God's Kingdom, who have tremendous potential to fulfill our purpose to bring glory to His name by the lives we live.

Esther experienced the JOY of God's presence through embracing difficult circumstances. Oswald Chambers calls this the "delight of despair." Catherine Marshall's book, *Something More*, teaches about "the Sacrifice of Praise."

Oftentimes, I coach myself with the phrase "acceptance with JOY." These words bring me before the King, where I can cast my cares at His feet. Like a potent balm of peace, JOY flows in and I find freedom.

There is nothing more powerful than experiencing God's mighty hand lifting our heads, empowering us to take our eyes off of our "human experience." In His presence we are able to walk with Him in the garden, far above the earthly circumstances in which we may find ourselves.

What JOY it is to gain His heavenly perspective, and then to actively apply it, like a verb, to every area of our lives.

Pray

Father, thank You for using my earthly experiences to draw me into Your presence. I pray Your Holy Spirit will immediately prompt me to offer You the sacrifice of praise; surrendering my human mind and thanking You instead! Forgive my unbelief, my doubt of Your timing, for questioning Your ways, and for passively sitting on the sidelines of my life. Thank You for my trials. I want the JOY of Your presence as I seek and trust You. There is nothing I desire more than being in alignment with You, to wholeheartedly enjoy the JOY of Your Kingdom life here on earth. Amen

The Joy Journal

Rachel Scott

But the Holy Spirit produces this kind of fruit in our lives…joy.
GALATIANS 5:22

When my four children were ages 15, 10, 7 and 4, we attended a church where the pastor encouraged us to set a goal to have a happy home. He inspired us through positive sermons on relationships, the fruits of the spirit, goal setting and seeking God's heart in our walks with Jesus. During that time, I was inspired to find clever ways to instill our family value system. One day an idea popped into my mind and it was to start something my children later called the "Joy Journal."

I bought a black and white speckled notebook, and at night while we were eating dinner, I started going around the table asking each child to share one positive thought about their day.

At first, I wasn't even sure this was going to be a good idea but much to our surprise the Joy Journal carved out a whole new chapter in our lives. The joy journal gave each child an opportunity to have *"their time to talk"*. In a family of four children, sometimes one or two children dominate the conversations while the quieter children remain silent. Yet with the Joy Journal each person got an opportunity to speak.

We would hear all kinds of stories about their friends, field trips, their co-op teachers, art class and after-school events, etc.

Many nights their insights were priceless, often hilarious and rarely predictable. Sometimes while I was writing down their thoughts, I would doodle a small picture about their event. They loved this especially when it was something funny that had happened and seeing my goofy artwork made the event even funnier. We would laugh so hard our sides would ache. Thus the "joy" we were seeking.

Over time we could see God working in our children's hearts, as before we started this ritual they might not have given their day a second thought. But by sharing events in front of our family, they really tried to figure out the best part of their day instead of simply wanting to talk. We could see positive growth happening.

One afternoon the girls grabbed the book and started cutting up photos and pasting them to the cover. They informed me the black and white speckled notebook was ugly, and they wanted to make it look pretty. The pictures made it look like our family.

I could go on and on about the "joy" the Joy Journal brought, and I wish I could say we had continued it for twenty years. But instead we were only faithful to the idea for a few years.

My husband started traveling, and he was often not home for dinner and our older son's sports and music activities meant he was not around much either. We tried to keep the idea alive, but one day we simply stopped writing in the journal and laid the idea to rest.

My first four children are now grown and several have babies. Sometimes when they're all together, they talk about the joy journal and wonder why we ever quit the idea. They'll get it out and read it, and the laughter begins all over again. They like to read about who their friends were and what they thought was important "back then" — especially which toys they were excited about or how the dumbest things seemed important. We always end up laughing. They regret we quit and tell me it was a highlight and an idea they want to do with their own children. When I hear this I smile inside!

Start a joy journal with your own family. It's never too late to start seeking positive thoughts about your day. We all have a story to share, and this may be why the joy journal will remain as one of the greatest highlights of my family's life.

Pray

Lord, today I pause to give thanks for my family. Today, let's open up to each other. Open our eyes to the joys and blessings that can be found in each day. Amen

Day 16

Joy of Discipleship

Marie Drakulic

Jesus came and told his disciples, "I have been given all authority in heaven and on earth. Therefore, go and make disciples of all the nations..." MATTHEW 28:18-19A

Something miraculous happened at my house. Our church's women's ministry met at my house for breakfast and Bible study. You may think this sounds mundane, but that couldn't be further from the truth. You see, in between bites of pancakes and sips of coffee, discipleship was happening.

In the little over a year since we began our ladies' Bible study, I have come to love these women as my own family. They have been a blessing to me in so many ways—helping, praying, encouraging, laughing, relating, fellowshipping, sharing . . . the list goes on. Yet, possibly my favorite thing about this group of women is their willingness to be so brutally honest. They aren't afraid to ask the tough questions, and they are truly seeking the answers.

I often think of Phillip when he asked in Acts 8:30, "Do you understand what you are reading?" Only, I feel so helpless sometimes to answer their questions. Sometimes, I have to honestly say, "I don't know." They challenge me to dig deeper into God's word and seek His face. Their burdens have become my burdens, and these wonderful women are constantly on my heart.

I could have no greater joy than to hear that my children are following the truth. 3 John 1:4

Although these women aren't my children, I feel abundant joy in seeing them grow in grace. Just thinking about them and how they have grown brings a smile to my face. Nothing makes me happier than to see them experience Christ in a very real and personal way!

I think of the grieving mother who is beginning to heal. I think of one who has served in the church for many years and is now seeing Christ move in new ways in her life. I think of a hurting mother who is learning to love her kids again.

It doesn't stop there.

The light of God is shining in these women's lives and is coming into their homes. God is using them to reach their families for His glory. So I rejoice in hearing that an unbelieving husband took his kids to church for the first time! I give praise to the Lord for the husband who has been saved and is now following in believer's baptism! What amazing joy I have in seeing a stony heart become softened by the gospel—the gospel that is being lived in *her* life!

What a privilege it is to be a part of something so incredible!

I am humbled in knowing that God chose me to lead them, to disciple them. At times, I feel inadequate. After all, I am far from perfect and my family has its own mess of problems. How could I possible help another when sometimes I don't know how to help myself? I find hope and encouragement from Jesus' words in the book of Luke, *What is impossible for people is possible with God* (18:27). By becoming a vessel for God to use, He can work through me to do works greater than I. And that is exactly what He did.

As our time drew to a close that day, I challenged the ladies (myself included) to "be Jesus with skin on." It is the same challenge I present to you today. Someone you know (or will soon meet) needs to see Jesus in your life. There may be a family member, a friend, a neighbor, or a person in your church that is hurting and searching for some answers.

Don't expect to have all the answers--God *can* and *wants* to use YOU in their life. He is calling you to surrender your will to His purposes. When you allow Him to take the brokenness of your own life into His capable hands, He can do something far greater than you can imagine!

Discipleship is a beautiful thing!

Pray

Lord, You have called me to be a disciple. Not only to grow in You, but to learn from others. We were made for community. Thank You for my friends who bring me such joy in life on earth. Amen

Loving Life: it's Your Choice

Casey Herringshaw

Do you love your life?

Don't answer this right away.

I'll come back around to the question. But I want you to really think this one through.

When you pause and look at your life and realize what surrounds you in this world, do you open your eyes and hear with a sense of awe? Or do you quickly pass on by, scurrying to the next task on your to-do list?

I can be just as guilty of this as the next gal. Life is busy. It's full of tasks and duties, chores and responsibilities that fill our hours and days with often mundane *things*.

It's easy to get sucked into the to-dos. The job, the home world, and the outside world that pulls us down with the evil that surrounds us on a minute-to-minute basis. Remaining positive—loving life—in a negative world—can sometimes be the hardest thing I do. And I'm not always successful.

Because, let's face it: life isn't always positive, and it's hard to always be positive about life. But we *can* make the choice to *love life* when we put the right perspective into place.

Do you take part in an activity, simply because you love doing it? Do you take the time to pause, even for just a moment and dance with your child (or if you're like me: by yourself?).

Do you smile often? Laugh much? We're told in Proverbs 31, this woman can *"laugh without fear of the future."*

Could such be said of you? Truly, take time to think through this question: *do you take time to laugh?*

When we have our eyes wide open to what is around us, when we allow the good things in life to fill us up as gifts from the hand of God, really, all the bad things in life start to fade away. This life we have? It's only temporary. It's a shell, not even a glimpse of the understanding of rewards that await God's children in Heaven.

Do you live life like that promise is yours? Because it is. This earthly body? You're just passing through on the way to the Kingdom of God.

When you take the time to intentionally love life, you open yourself up to the joy that surrounds you on a daily basis.

How can you change your mind set toward this love and joy of life?

• Take time for prayer every day with God. During your commute, while you make breakfast, prepare for the day, etc. Start your day off with intentional time with God.

• Make a point to notice the little things. The change in fall colors. The twinkle in your child's eye. The beauty of your surroundings.

• Let. It. Go. Release the strangle hold you have on the circumstances you can't control. Open your eyes to the work God is doing in your life and the goodness He gives you in every moment.

- Take the time to dance to the music. Smile to the sound of birds. Laugh at the days to come. And the silly things that happen within the moments.

So, I'll return to my earlier question: do you love life?

It's an intentional decision, and not something that just happens. But when you make that choice -- and purposefully put it into action -- it'll change your life.

Pray

God, I feel stuck sometimes. The day-to-day grind can bring me down. Help me to remember that You are there, even in the mundane tasks of life, and that You have a purpose for me. Amen

Day 18

Not When, But Now

Lori Clapper

I have put off joy for too long. Oh, I've had a lot of laughs and good times throughout my life. But buried beneath the outward smiles, there was always something missing. I didn't experience joy in the moment. When it counted, I thought joy would only come when:

...we could move to a bigger house.

...I got that better job.

...the holidays would come and we had some shiny new things.

...I could keep my house clean for more than an hour.

Quite honestly, these "whens" can kill your spirit and squelch any chance for joy. But I am realizing that now, in hindsight. And I want to encourage you:

You *can* enjoy your life. *Right now.*

I don't mean you can't have those things. God designed us to have dreams and goals, and He wants nothing more than to incredibly bless us. In fact, His word says He can provide anything we need, according to His riches. But don't focus so much on those things that you can't be still and love the life you have at this moment. You can have joy that can change the course of your life. Right now, joy can:

Give you the strength you need: Nehemiah 8:10 *Don't be dejected and sad, for the joy of the LORD is your strength!"*

Make you free to enjoy your life: *The thief's purpose is to steal and kill and destroy. My purpose is to give them a rich and satisfying life.* John 10:10

Allow you to really celebrate: *So go ahead. Eat your food with joy, and drink your wine with a happy heart, for God approves of this!* Ecclesiastes 9:7

Grow your faith in God: *…and though you have not seen Him, you love Him, and though you do not see Him now, but believe in Him, you greatly rejoice with joy inexpressible and full of glory, obtaining as the outcome of your faith the salvation of your souls.* 1 Peter 1:8-9

Today, choose joy.

Pray

Lord, thank You that You are the only source of our true joy. I want to only fix my eyes on You today, so I can live life to the full and enjoy my life, where You have me.

Day 19

Peace in Chaos

Lori Clapper

Then Jesus said, "Come to me, all of you who are weary and carry heavy burdens, and I will give you rest. Take my yoke upon you. Let me teach you, because I am humble and gentle at heart, and you will find rest for your souls. For my yoke is easy to bear, and the burden I give you is light." MATTHEW 11:28-30

Re-location.

That was the first step in my plan to bust the clutter that had built up in my house during the past month or so. Jam-packed weekends and evenings led to my family being home for just enough time to make messes and not much time to *really* clean them up again.

So last weekend, I stood up to my challenge — taking a deep breath, rolling up my sleeves and arming myself with cleaning sprays and paper towels.

I started in the kitchen where I knew I had a breakfast bar somewhere under the piles of mail and school papers. I gathered everything — every last paper, bill, toy and straggling bottle of nail polish — and plopped them down in the back playroom. With the clutter out of sight, I could then concentrate on scrubbing everything down until it sparkled. It took hours, but I went from room to room, repeating that same exercise and making the visible area of my home as neat as a pin. My house hadn't looked this great in what seemed like ages. *Except for the back room.*

The heaps of "miscellaneous" grew, along with toys that were already there. "This will take a bit more focused time," I thought to myself, tired out after hours of hard work. "I'll deal with that later…." *It's hidden, anyway. Right?*

This made me think about our hearts. It's oftentimes too easy to just hide the emotional clutter in an effort to look like you have it all together. Like my playroom, you hope nobody explores too far to see what is really going on.

But buried deep within us are hurt feelings, jealousy or anger or perhaps actions done in secret such as an affair, abuse or an abortion. Re-located. Built up. Cluttering the deepest recesses of our hearts and minds. Waiting to be dealt with. We keep it to ourselves, however in the meantime it impacts our lives emotionally, mentally and physically.

Truth is, God is patiently waiting for us to give our struggles over to Him. He never judges and always heals. Most of all, He guarantees the peace you seek. You don't have to have it all together. He says to come just as you are...

Hurting.

Disappointed.

Overwhelmed.

Cluttered with the stuff of life.

Remind yourself of what Jesus says in Matthew 11:28-30 – *we need to give our heavy burdens over to God.*

Speak God's words of peace and joy over your life. Embrace it. Confess your "stuff" to Him. Find a trustworthy friend and tell her about the challenges you face, pray over it together and bring them into the light. Then you will discover HIS peace that surpasses all understanding, even in the midst of your chaos.

Pray

Lord, I pray for Your peace today. For I know that joy and peace go hand in hand. And when I know Your peace in my heart, I can truly find joy. Amen

Day 20

Prodigal

Janelle Keith

Dear God, show me what it means to follow You. May my heart's response be as pure and always full of praise as the mother of Jesus. You so graciously give visual confirmations that You care for me. May my heart always believe in You, and not be distracted by my own understanding or doubts, fears and tears. May I always and forever say yes to You and the joy ahead for me. And yes, with whole faith God, not based on visual evidence, but on the faith and trust that only comes from You. It's You Jesus, only You. May I always say yes to You. Amen.

(From my prayer journal...raw and unedited...)

I want to write 1000 sentences all at once. And yet, I can't seem to get all of the words out. You know the incredible and unbelievable desires I have in my soul. May I delight myself in You Jesus? Certainly, when I think about You, what You mean to me well...my eyes get misty and my heart flutters. Lord I have been talking to You about my prodigal.

I never would have thought that in my "someday"...my dreams of becoming a mom that...God...this would happen to our family and that one of our own would go astray. I'm so afraid to say it out loud to You or anyone else. Have I messed up as a mother? Have I led my child astray? Such pain in seeing the child go the wrong way and yet You remind me of Your shepherding love?

I want to remember real joy of holding this now grown child like I was holding onto this precious one when they were born. This is way beyond what I had planned. But God You know my heart's desire is to submit to You, follow You and obey what You have asked of me. May I continue to love this child, even though they stray from You. I am moved by Your relentless care of me so that I can't help but be relentless in my love and care for those -- even though they fall out of fellowship with You Lord.

Your care and concern for me overwhelmed me to Your peace-filled pastures. I am speechless yet overflowing with joy that I have never felt before.

This peace and joy quickens my soul. Your joy is complete and feels so alive with Your Hope. But God this is so strange, different and awkward. Give me more grace to receive this blessing, this favor, this whole love that compels me to love in the messy of this family's life. It's such a burden to pray continually for Your work in my prodigal's life. I want to remember this joy feeling is my healing forever, this moment of awe, and anticipation of Your greatness. Help me prepare for what is ahead. I can see some fearful moments, some scary steps, but what I want to see is faith opportunities for You to work and strengthen my faith. Help me to prepare, to be ready and deepen my joy. My heart can't get past Mary's own agonizing moments when she watched Your son Jesus die for all of us, for me, for those who put her Son on a cruel cross. There is no way a mother could have joy in such agonizing days, but yet she must have.

I must remember to choose joy when I don't see it. I want to remember those words.... highly favored by the Holy One, therein lies my joy in finding Your favor. May my lips magnify Your Holy Name with joy when I don't feel it. Jesus, the Son of the Most High. I want to remember Your words forever! Oh my heart wants to sing this song forever when I remember the joy of the cross.

Again, my heart overflows with worship now. I believe in the power of miracles. I believe in these joyless and pain-filled days that bring me joy in remembering pure joy is from above.

God You are giving life to my dreams, my heart, soul, my joy and hope. Please accept my joy of praise as an offering to You, Oh Lord...may it be just like Mary's response, let these words of her heart, soak into my prodigal seasons and days... May the prodigals out there searching for love see Your love in the most joy filled way.

Luke 1:47-49 *How my spirit rejoices in God my Savior! For he took notice of his lowly servant girl, and from now on all generations will call me blessed. For the Mighty One is holy, and he has done great things for me.*

Pray

Oh Lord, You have remembered Your people, You have found favor, You have restored my joy! May it be as You have said...Your servant, ~ yes, even me, mother of a prodigal, that these days will be restored unto Thee.... with a perfect joy! Amen

Day 21

Salty Tears, Trickles of Joy

Holly Smith

Life is full of the bittersweet. Live long enough and we are sure to experience grief, joy and at times a medley of the two. I will always remember when my family, having lost my dad to a long physical battle, sat around our dining room table to plan his going home service.

Dad was intentional and clear about this being a day of celebration. Amongst the details he had jotted down on a yellow-lined legal pad, he wrote that those of us reading his well-planned order of service should not be sad but rejoice, for he was now with the Lord.

That was a true "salty tears, trickles of joy moment" that, for me, echoed throughout the entire grieving process. It was that combination of emotions that I found to be a great source of comfort. The confidence in knowing that my daddy is now whole and free in the presence of Jesus did then, and still does, cause my heart to leap.

I recall the heartfelt and tender moments of conversation with dear friends and loved ones that day, and I can honestly say that despite my grief, my spirit celebrated. I have never liked funeral homes. But the little open, sunlit area where we all gathered to visit that week, had a beautiful, lightly stain-glassed window. Rays of sunshine just poured into that room. The presence of the Holy Spirit was evident in every way. Dad had run his race with perseverance and had received his prize; And my heart did indeed burst with songs of thanksgiving. I will always be grateful for the ability to see so much joy through the tears. It is my prayer that you also, my beloved, will know the immense joy that His presence and promises of eternity bring.

Pray

Father, we thank You today for the joy that we have in You. Your joy makes us complete. You help us in all situations and no matter the circumstance, we can have true joy because of You. We thank You and we celebrate today! Amen

Day 22

Speak Life

Janelle Keith

When she speaks, her words are wise, and she gives instructions with kindness. PROVERBS 31:26

Here's what I have found out about being kind - it brings a joy that won't be found otherwise. Kindness uproots a hidden joy that is only given by love. And when we realize how loved and appreciated we are to the Father, then we can't help but be joyful, right? Did you know there is joy in forgiveness?

There is great joy and liberation in forgetfulness too.

A kind word is a seed, which often bears fruit in joy. You see we don't know what path others are walking along. We don't know what is happening behind their closed doors. We don't know their story, but we do know what we have to deal with daily. When pain has worn us down and those we meet hold onto anger and rejection, their joy is simply not obvious is it?

You can tell by their faces, their worry, the fear, and the pain that they choose to wear. We wear our emotions whether we know it or not. And it hides behind those unkind words, those cold looks, those sad smiles and sighs. Why do we hide our joy so readily when it's the very thing that speaks volumes about our faith so steadily? My friend's husband struggles through the pain of cancer and she smiles. How? My friend's daughter just miscarried again, and you could hear her joy through the phone?

My pastor knows someone who just buried a child and they expressed their joy at the funeral?

Doesn't joy only have its right place to dance for babies and at weddings?

No, joy belongs everywhere God is. God is joy and part of the fruit He bears in us, not to only be chosen for births announcements and wedding receptions. As our lives go, joy gives and grows...and joy multiplies joy.

Let me explain further.

A kind word makes a difference. And what this world needs are more kind words towards each other.

A kind word gifts joy. Try it sometime...you too will be amazed at the response. Seriously, have you ever just thanked someone for doing something that they normally do? Have you made them feel significant in any way? Joy chooses kindness, especially in the vehicle of words.

You will be surprised what a hurting world will do when it is met with joy and kindness. Choosing joy is bonding and strengthening. Joy seeds smiles, and laughter. Joy heals wounds that can't be expressed openly. Hurt people hurt people. Jesus is the pure example of intruding on the hurting world in the face of rejection and hatred. It didn't stop Him, so it shouldn't stop us.

The joy of the Lord is contagious, and restoring, and oh so healing! Be kind. Choose some joyful words, like you have lost your mind. Go over the top in spreading it. We tend to cling to the negative and forget the positive. We all need reminders of joy, in every way and every day. Try it ....it works!

Now practice...say something joyful even if it is raining. Dance in the rain like you just don't care. Jesus always has joy for us, we delight Him, we need to acknowledge that and give that kind of surprising joy to someone else!

Choosing joy is an option, speaking life is a gift, giving gifts is our privilege to point the joy -filled way to Christ.

Pray

Father, I pray for opportunities to speak life and share the joy You've given to me. It's truly a gift to be shared with others. Let it overflow to those around me today. Amen

Day 23

The Holy Spirit Welcome Mat

Patti Orton Kuna

...He will rejoice over you with joyful songs.
ZEPHANIAH 3:17

Did you ever notice how a hectic lifestyle actually inhibits us from receiving joy? We wake up, slurp down some breakfast while our minds are already in the car anticipating the commute. We work all day only to come home to find more work: preparing dinner, dishes, laundry, homework, and extracurricular activities. Then we brush our teeth and collapse in bed, barely recouping long enough in order to push through again tomorrow. Where and when is the joy? We don't give the Holy Spirit a chance living this kind of lifestyle.

Conversely, did you ever notice how newborn babies are never humdrum? Might part of that reason be because we put the brakes on our high-speed minds and feet to observe, admire and contemplate the miracle? It is not a coincidence that we are uplifted with joy when we cuddle such a gift. No, the quieted mind is like a welcome mat and a cup of tea for the Holy Spirit to visit, linger and bestow joy upon us.

Indeed, there is a strong correlation between quietness of the mind and joy. The first preempts the other.

Because joy is not something we can manufacture, we need to decelerate in order to receive it, in full form, from the Holy Spirit. It is not until we pause, breathe and embrace who or what is before us, do we open ourselves like a flower to catch the vitalizing dew of joy.

Though we cannot manufacture it, joy needn't be happenstance either. We needn't wait for newborn babies to cross our paths. There are miracles and blessings all around us every day that we mistakenly gloss over. A lime green leaf, a summer toad, the sunrise that never duplicates – there are endless God-given jewels all around us every day reminding us to get quiet, marvel and put down our Holy Spirit welcome mat.

Lest there be confusion, the gift of joy is not mere happiness. Joy is an elevating, permeating sensation with the capacity to remove you from the cares of this world - but not in a phony way. Rather, in a way that straight out verifies the holy presence of the Living God, and a perceptible, humbling kinship with Him. Happiness is a human pursuit. Joy is a holy sampling of heaven.

Pray

Dear Heavenly Father, discipline me to pause throughout my days to contemplate the innumerable miracles that surround me. Help me learn to quiet my mind deliberately thereby welcoming Your Holy Spirit to uplift me in joy. Through Jesus Christ I pray, Amen

Day 24

The Water Bottle

Rachel Scott

For the Kingdom of God is not a matter of what we eat or drink,
but of living a life of goodness and peace and joy in the Holy Spirit.
ROMANS 14:17

My 8th grade daughter needed to make an end of the school year gift for the girls on her sports team. As usual, the team waited until the very last minute. The gifts were supposed to get everyone excited about the state championships, which was at the end of the week. They could have told us a month ago, but the team captain forgot to mention it so instead the gift was needed in three days. When I found out, I was just coming off of a weekend engagement, had not unpacked yet and was swamped with errands and work.

I was forced to switch gears, jump in the car and run my daughter out to find water bottles in her team colors. The committee decided a cute gift would be plastic water bottles filled with candy, a personal monogram on the side, a decorative label and some curling ribbon. A very cute idea, but to find the water bottles in her team colors of orange or blue at the last minute meant we might encounter some problems. When we went shopping, all we could find were bottles in every other color. Feeling rushed and exasperated, we purchased red bottles instead of blue or orange and for $3.00 each. It was the best we could find.

My daughter went to practice, and I agreed to go to pick up the monograms at my girlfriend's house. She was doing a similar project for her daughter's school. When I arrived I saw her purchase. She had found water bottles at the dollar store (of all places) and hers were in beautiful pastels. When I remarked at her "find", she told me they had tons of blue bottles. So being the good mother that I am, I decided to surprise her and run to the dollar store to get her the blue bottles. Of course when I got there they were sold out of the blue, but they said that they had them at their other store six miles away — down a very busy road during rush-hour traffic. I surmised that I would go ahead and drive down there since I had another errand in that same direction.

When I finally arrived, they were all sold out of blue like the kind we wanted but instead I grabbed a similar water bottle. I figured I had done my *good mom* deed for the day. When I got home and showed them to her she was so excited for the blue. However, this bottle was shaped differently, and the monogram label did not look good on the bottle! Ugh! The next day I had to go back to the dollar store and exchange those bottles for the pastel water bottles that were shaped correctly. Oh my, what a hassle that was — and all for a silly piece of plastic!

Afterwards, as I was reflecting on one day in my life as a mom, I think I was feeling happy we pulled it off, but also a tad exasperated about the hassle of items selling out before I got there and the trouble it always seems to take to get one little thing done. The amount of money, time and aggravation

I spent seems like wasted energy. In the end we did get the cute water bottles, yet the whirlwind of life caused me to not en-"joy" something as simple as helping my daughter find her supplies.

I don't think I am always "enjoying life" like I should; some days everything is a hassle, and nothing is fun. I realize that God did not put me here with the primary goal of enjoying life and that sometimes life will give me hard things. But whatever is thrown my way it is my attitude towards those things that God cares about.

Romans 14:17 says: *For the kingdom of God is not a matter of eating or drinking but of righteousness peace and joy in the Holy Spirit.* In this verse it says that the kingdom of God means that I reflect the Lord whenever I encounter life's trials and should be reflecting His peace and His joy, rather than react to life with a poor attitude.

This verse spoke to my heart. God cares about me maintaining my attitude of joy. I need to view each day as an opportunity to allow Him to flow through me and to keep a smile on my face and joy in my heart no matter what life throws me!

Pray

Lord, when life throws me a curve ball, I pray your strength and courage to keep a healthy attitude and to not forget to keep Your joy in the center of it all. Amen

Day 25

When Joy is Hard to Find

Janelle Keith

Everything has its wonders, even darkness and silence, and I learn,
whatever state I may be in, therein to be content.

~Helen Keller

Joy soon slips from our grasp once we have experienced it, and it often seems that it plays hide and seek with our hearts. Why is the gift of joy so hard to see, to feel, to experience? Can we find true contentment for our hearts and in our lives?

In the joyless world we live in, it seems harder and harder to find, not to mention to grasp a hold of.

If the success of our day or the joy of our mood is dictated by everything going our way, or hitting the green light and not getting stuck in traffic on the interstate. If you are looking for joy in these places, you won't find it there. How deeply rooted can we be in the love of Christ when our gift of joy is sucked from our lips with something as simple as missing a green light or letting the slightest disappointment, completely derail us? Or when plans don't work out like we expected and we quickly escalate to a fit of rage and fury?

It's funny that we think we can handle adversity or trials when we can't even handle the check-out line at the local market! God grows our character through testing and hardship. I wonder what it looks like to Him when we can't even handle the gas station pumps that don't automatically lock forcing you to stand there and hold the trigger in!

There is no joy in those scenarios that I just described but you can have a joyful attitude in the disappointments of life. Can we really claim to be filled with God's love and joy only to have it dissolve when our expectations disintegrate because of an email that shouldn't have been sent?

I think what makes having a discontent heart tough is that it sneaks up on you. It starts with something small and it grows. It grows and starts to form a bitter root that consumes over time, seeping into all areas of your life. Before you know it, you forget what joy is, and how it feels.

If anyone has a true reason to be discontent with the way their life turned out, it would be those who empathize with Helen Keller. She may not have been able to hear or see but she believed that she could be happy and content in any situation. Do you notice the difference in her world and yours?

The difference was in her perspective of the darkness. Helen's darkness was dark no matter what and nothing was going to change that, but she knew she COULD change her perspective of it.

If Helen could find wonder in the darkness and silence, then how much more can we as Christians find joy and wonder in the dark places of our lives. If Helen could find contentment in the silence she lived in, then how much more should we find our hearts happy.

Being deeply rooted in Christ, we can have access to a joy that nothing in this life can take away. By putting our trust and faith in God alone we are able to endure any situation no matter how painful it may be. By understanding that we are here to worship God through life and spread the truth of His love; rather than Him being here to grant our desires and wishes. We are granted the ability to find joy in any situation that life throws at us.

Philippians 4:11 ... *Not that I was ever in need, for I have learned how to be content with whatever I have.*

Paul knew true joy and lived it.

There is nothing on this planet that is greater than God. There is no problem that can take away God's love for us, or the unspeakable joy that comes from being in His presence. There is no situation that causes God to be afraid and remove Himself from it. We are granted the right and the privilege to be carriers of joy as we sit in traffic, stand in line at Wal-Mart, get overlooked at work, get taken advantage of by friends, or live with noisy roommates.

Our hearts should not be discontent because of our circumstances.

Our unhappiness is evidence that we have not given up our own expectations nor fully surrendered ourselves to God. When we fully surrender our lives to God, we become adaptable to any situation and usable at God's choosing.

A life of joy rooted in the peace that comes from being content with Christ and His plans for us is not a life that is rooted in how good life treats us. When we are unhappy with the things in our life then we are unhappy with the one who placed us around those things. Always remember that to surrender your life to Christ is to live in the constant wonder, amazement, and joy of who He is and the price He paid with His own blood for our lives. His joy that His presence gives is what you are looking for!

Pray

Father, remind me of the good that can be found in every circumstance. My prayer is to live Your joy through learning contentment in life. Amen

Day 26

Warm Woolen Mittens

Holly Smith

You will show me the way of life, granting me the joy of your presence and the pleasures of living with you forever. PSALM 16:11

"Raindrops on roses and whiskers on kittens; Bright copper kettles and warm woolen mittens..." I totally adore this never forgotten and will-be-forever-loved scene from the musical *The Sound of Music*.

During a bedtime storm, Julie Andrews remarkably sings and dances away the children's fears. Her notes, accompanied by thoughts of whimsy and all that is dreamy, take the children from fright to freedom. Their focus shifts from claps of thunder and wild streaks of blinding lightning to simple things that bring joy.

I love simplicity. Diamonds on a sandy beach and curtains blowing in the ocean breeze...cherished times with trusted friends...giving and receiving kisses and love from my furry canine children...I love it all.

We live in a world of fast and furious. Fifteen minutes is a long time to wait for food, coffee brews in like 10 seconds, and when people say "How are you?" -- they really aren't expecting anything other than "Good, how are you?"

Success is duly measured by how much we accomplish, not according to our own standards. Rather it's measured against the unobtainable standards of others.

Operating in a rush-rush, hub-to-hub, I'm losing my mind kind of existence is exhausting. And let's face it, can be downright debilitating.

When it comes to experiencing joy, this type of full-speed ahead journey with no stops for air, leaves us depleted. It is indeed valuable to take time for rest and renewal. We can't even begin to tap into such joy, however, if we don't slow down enough to embrace the moment.

What brings you joy? I don't know if for you it is wiggling your toes in the sand or taking a super-charged nap. But I do know one thing for sure, and that is: *There is more. Much more.* As we journey through life as women living in a growing and personal relationship with Jesus Christ, we so desperately need to know and experience joy in all its fullness. In order to get to the True Source of joy, we need to be still. Basking in His presence, listening for His voice through His Word and in prayer, and embracing and loving those around us are the best things a girl could ask for.

When you feel dry, when you feel happy, when you are restless or ridiculously tired...whatever your state of mind, run to Him, beloved, for He is The Joy-Keeper. I stand with you this day, praying and believing for the fullness of God to fill your mind and heart to overflowing until it can't be contained anymore!

Pray

God, I ask that You will fill me with all joy and peace in believing, that by the power of Your Holy Spirit, my heart would abound and be overflowing (bubbling over) with hope. Amen

Day 27

Joy in a Jar

Holly Smith

I pray that God, the source of hope, will fill you completely with joy and peace because you trust in him. Then you will overflow with confident hope through the power of the Holy Spirit. ROMANS 15:13

When wanting to remember an answer to prayer, how do you capture it? Maybe you collect items that represent each provision and tuck them away in a pretty box for the treasure they are, or maybe you write them on the pages of a beautifully bound journal.

I have done both. Whether it is on little note cards held together by twine, in a beach glass jar, or on antiqued papyrus bound by leather, the purpose remains the same.

We want to be able to go back in time and reflect upon the "oh so goodness" of the God we serve and trust. Sometimes we share testimonies of His blessings with others, to encourage them through a difficult place in their journey.

Other times we need a refreshing reminder ourselves, especially when we find ourselves in a place called the unknown, where fear tends to rear its ugly head. I need that, even in this very moment as I write to you. And then sometimes we just want to reminisce, giving God thanksgiving for His faithfulness.

I have many joy-in-a-jar moments that cause my heart to leap when I think upon them. Like the time when I needed 75 dollars to pay my book fees at college, and a lady at my church gave me a cookie tin full of coins equaling the exact amount. Or how faithful prayers every night kept our old farmhouse church parsonage from burning down when in the natural it should have. When my family moved to pastor a new church, and they went in to inspect the old house, my parents were told it was nothing short of a miracle that the wiring had not caused a fire or that the furnace had not exploded.

I will never forget the time when my dad recovered from a serious, life-threatening infection. Or when my brother was healed from an intestinal disease and when I, too, was healed. The list goes on.

I encourage you, my sweet beloved sister, to take moments to remember and praise God for all that He has done for you. He is a faithful God. I claim and believe that today, for us both.

Pray

Heavenly Father, we thank You from the core of our very beings for WHO You are. You are our Provider, our Healer, and our Friend. Jesus, You give us Life, the greatest of all joys and hem us in behind and before. Your Holy Spirit comforts and brings joy. We love You today and give You all glory due. Amen

Day 28

Joy in a Season of Rest

Janelle Keith

It was a season that I was unprepared for and didn't know what it would look like, though it was exactly what I needed. I had just given my all at a job for 13 and a half years and had resigned my position to pursue full-time writing. My new season wasn't exactly what I had signed up for.

Honestly I didn't know what it would look like except it felt good to sleep in past 3:45 am. That was my wake-up call as I was the co-host on a radio morning show. I did have some expectations going into this new thing that God was doing in me. I was ready for a change. I thought it would be easy. I thought it be great and grand. I thought I was already prepared. I thought a lot of things.

I didn't think it would look lonely, or leave me with a feeling of insignificance or leave me feeling marginal in any way. I didn't realize I needed any rest and could transition to one season to the next. I didn't know that I would need to see any results to feel productive. I didn't think it would be so hard to discover my purpose.

This new place was about the exact opposite of my previous work environment. May I be a bit transparent here? I felt a bit weak in this type of rest. I thought I knew what this was about, but God showed me that there were more important things to accomplish as I prepared for the coming season.

Have I told you that I have a hard time standing still? It's difficult for me to rest. I didn't realize how worn out I really was. Emotionally I didn't realize how spent I was on the inside. The transition from a very public personality to a full-time writer was challenging for me. You see, I am a people person. I used to talk to people for my job, and the moment I left that position, intense isolation and loneliness set in.

I remember feeling so unproductive in my newfound season for rest. I could hardly wait for God to launch the next step of His grand plan for me. I believed it was around the corner, but at the same time, I missed people in a painful way.

So I asked God where was His joy in this resting. Where's the joy in my feeling isolated? Where was His joy in my new, yet unfamiliar freedom?

Because I was dealing with doubt, I re-evaluated my decision again and again. Because I was looking for the fruits of my labor everywhere, I lost my motivation to share my weight loss story in book form. Because I didn't see His purpose of what I wrote about, I couldn't find the joy in my freedom.

It was a couple of months in, when I realized that God was working on His time frame not mine. I slowly began to regain a right trust for His timetable.

My preparation season was stilling my heart's desire before the Lord. Only He knew I needed that before projecting me into the next phase of this writing journey.

He knew that I needed to build strength as a writer. He knew I needed a new dose of hope, and He knew that my confidence needed some encouragement. He knew what I needed even though I kept telling Him what I wanted.

I often think about how we try to jump ahead of God or try to produce our own little spin on His great purpose for our lives. There are days that I wonder what God is up to, but I know I can trust Him to meet my needs more than I can supply the words to wrap around them.

I am mostly left in wonder that my Father, who has no needs, can anticipate all of mine no matter the season.

Once I realized I could trust Him in my newfound season of rest, I felt His release to my new phase of ministry.

Once I realized that I was stepping into my calling, I received the joy that He had waiting for me.

Once I realized that I was never alone on any day, whether it was a public setting or not, I sensed His presence in a way that I can't describe.

Once I realized I found joy in my freedom, I felt peace that passes my understanding.

Once I dropped my expectations of what my life should look like, healing came like rain from heaven.

I saw the fruits of my labor, and I stepped into my purpose as His daughter.

I took my place in the kingdom and never doubted again. Finding His joy in the freedom of your calling is a beautiful thing and helps define your identity in so many ways. Finding purpose for your life is joyful, finding rest in due seasons is healing, and finding a deep trust that empowers your faith is life changing.

Pray

Father, in this world, busy-ness equals productivity...which translates into so-called "success." Thank You for teaching me how much You can accomplish through me in seasons of rest. And that I can find joy in the calm shelter of Your arms. Amen

Day 29

Joy When God Seems Far Away

Lori Clapper

In my recent prayer times, Psalm Seventy-Seven has come to mind. The Lord led me to this passage a couple of months ago when I took a day to fast and pray. And I feel in my heart that you may need these words as much as I did then (and still do today). So my hope and deepest prayer is that *your* heart will be encouraged to trust God in your circumstances. Right now. Just where you are.

I cry out to God; yes, I shout.

Oh, that God would listen to me!

When I was in deep trouble,

I searched for the Lord.

All night long I prayed, with hands lifted toward heaven,

but my soul was not comforted.

I think of God, and I moan,

overwhelmed with longing for his help.

You don't let me sleep.

I am too distressed even to pray!

I think of the good old days,

long since ended,

when my nights were filled with joyful songs.

I search my soul and ponder the difference now.

When you are walking in the valleys of life, it can seem endless, can't it?

I don't know what you're going through, but God knows how you feel. He understands your inner turmoil...how beaten down your spirit is. Have you run out of words to pray? Speaking your fears and troubles AGAIN seems like a waste of time because God has been silent. You question God's sovereignty and wonder if He has forgotten you.

Has the Lord rejected me forever?
Will he never again be kind to me?
Is his unfailing love gone forever?
Have his promises permanently failed?
Has God forgotten to be gracious?
Has he slammed the door on his compassion?

These questions may rip at your soul today. They are all too raw and familiar. Beloved, God is waiting for you. Do you remember the times God seemed so close -- "the good old days"? Before you throw up your hands in defeat, think on those things.

And I said, "This is my fate;
the Most High has turned his hand against me."
But then I recall all you have done, O Lord;
I remember your wonderful deeds of long ago.
They are constantly in my thoughts.
I cannot stop thinking about your mighty works.
O God, your ways are holy.
Is there any god as mighty as you?
You are the God of great wonders!
You demonstrate your awesome power among the nations.
By your strong arm, you redeemed your people...

His ways are holy. He is Great. Your Abba was a God of miracles, love, peace, mercy, grace and joy while you were on the mountaintop. And He never changes, even when the storms roll in. Remember His mighty deeds and the miracles of the past. Praise Him for all that He's done. And know today He is walking right beside you through all of it.

Pray

Father, thank You for scriptures that lead me into a deeper walk with You. Help me to recall all You've done in the past, but give me grace to see You moving today in my life. Amen

Day 30

Growing Some Joy Muscles

Karen Anna Vogel

I prayed over my grandson. "Lord, you healed Peter's mother-in-law of a fever. Please heal him."

He's still sick. I used to beat myself up, believing I don't have enough faith. But then there's the "James Factor" as I call it. *Dear brothers and sisters, when troubles of any kind come your way, consider it an opportunity for great joy. For you know that when your faith is tested, your endurance has a chance to grow. So let it grow, for when your endurance is fully developed, you will be perfect and complete, needing nothing…God blesses those who patiently endure testing and temptation. Afterward they will receive the crown of life that God has promised to those who love him.* JAMES 1:2-4, 12 (NLT)

Part two of the "James Factor" is a pastor in Haiti who taught me more about suffering and spiritual growth than anyone. While on a mission's trip to Dominican Republic to help displaced Haitians, I met Pastor James. He had walked with his two children from Haiti to Dominican Republic after his wife left him and returned to voodoo. This was a three-day hike at least. His kids were bone thin and their eyes hollow.

What did Pastor James talk about when he led a small prayer meeting? Joy in suffering. The way that our faith grows is through trials, he said. I was flabbergasted.

He was a walking talking object lesson. I cried on his shoulder when we had to return to the USA. "We don't have what you have here." It's true. Haitians have extreme faith and love, yet are the poorest people in the Western Hemisphere.

I want this kind of faith and endurance but then I shrink from trials, just like I shrink from exercise. They're both painful to me, but it's the way we grow muscle, spiritual and physical.

Pray

Lord, help me not shy away from trials. Give me eyes to see that hard times make my faith more solid. Amen

Day 31

Joy When You Don't Have a Minute

Lori Clapper

Go, eat your food with gladness, and drink your wine with a joyful heart, for it is now that God favors what you do. ECCLESIASTES 9:7

I was more than half way through my "year of joy." But I was starting to feel like the joy I was hoping for might in fact have an expiration date. My dreams of having extended time to pray and bask in the joy of the Lord were quickly dashed.

Instead, I found myself spending hours in the car, carting around kids to practices. I could barely keep up with my own work, let alone everyone else's stuff. With so many irons in the fire, my wear-with-all was just about wear-with-gone. I was growing weary. I didn't even have a minute to form a thought, let alone have any joy about it. "OK, God. This is supposed to be the year of joy. I didn't even make it to December," I prayed, feeling like a complete failure.

Then one day it hit me. In this season of life, I may not have hours of extra time. But God does give me the necessary minutes to find joy in different ways. I had to change my thoughts once again, adopting what Solomon wrote in Ecclesiastes: *Go eat your food with gladness, and drink your wine with a joyful heart, for it is now that God favors what you do.*

Now is the time. In your running around, washing the never-ending sink full of dishes, exercising when you're too tired, or fixing dinner for your family – don't waste those minutes annoyed and frustrated. They are all things you have to do, anyway. Right? So enjoy them! That is my challenge for you as you continue your joy habit. *Enjoy every moment.*

You might be thinking that it's not as easy as that three-word sentence might suggest. But if joy doesn't come easy for you, take baby steps each day.

Say a prayer for a friend after washing each dish. Use that exercise time to listen to an uplifting podcast or your favorite sing-along-able music. Those hours in the car? They can be teachable moments with your kids or quiet times to decompress from the day.

Inviting those intentional joy-building habits into your day will change your life. I promise. And more importantly God promises it, and He'll use those every-day moments to fill you with His joy, peace, and strength.

Pray

Lord, thank You for Your joy. It is truly a gift from You. Help me see the 'Joy Moments', even if it's for a few seconds. Give me grace to make joy a habit in my life. Amen

About Wonderfully WOVEN

Our Mission:

At **Wonderfully WOVEN**, we encourage women to find peace and purpose in their beautiful, imperfect lives.

Our Purpose:

At **Wonderfully WOVEN**, we believe that every woman is an exceptional fabric weaved together by the love she gives away, the intelligence she possesses and presents, the problems she faces, the courage she musters, the skills and strengths within herself and from others that she can access, her unique personality, her creative outlets, and the faith she places in the God who created her.

The Joy Habit
Contributing Authors

Lori Clapper

Marie Drakulic

Dr. Andrea Hazim

Casey Herringshaw

Janelle Keith

Patti Orton-Kuna

Tara Norman

Julia Reffner

Rachel Scott

Holly Smith

Karen Anna Vogel

Angie Webb

Please connect with us at:

http://www.wonderfullywoven.com

COVER DESIGN: Lori Clapper
KINDLE LAYOUT AND DESIGN: Karen Anna Vogel
PAPERBACK LAYOUT AND DESIGN: Dawn A. Estela

Made in the USA
San Bernardino, CA
16 June 2016